LIVING WITH A **BLACK** DOG

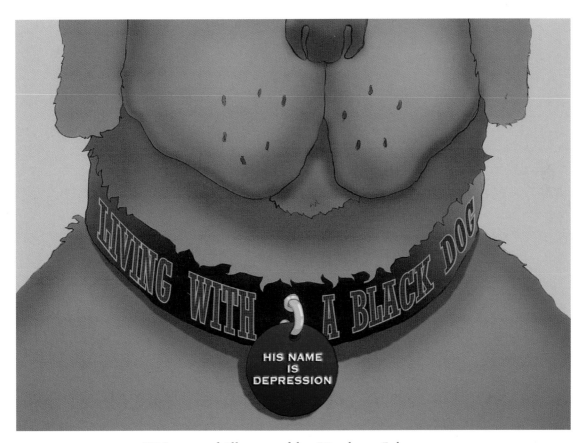

Written and Illustrated by Matthew Johnstone

**Andrews McMeel
Publishing, LLC**

Kansas City • Sydney • London

LIVING WITH A **BLACK** DOG

Andrews McMeel Publishing, LLC
an Andrews McMeel Universal company
1130 Walnut Street, Kansas City, Missouri 64106

www.andrewsmcmeel.com

11 12 13 14 15 WKT 10 9 8 7 6 5 4

ISBN: 978-0-7407-5743-3

ATTENTION: SCHOOLS AND BUSINESSES

Andrews McMeel books are available at quantity discounts with bulk purchase for
educational, business, or sales promotional use. For information, please e-mail the
Andrews McMeel Publishing Special Sales Department:
specialsales@amuniversal.com

(Not) for my family and friends

People who've had a Black Dog in their lives often say that in retrospect,
"the Dog" probably had been sniffing around for a long time.
They just didn't have the understanding and knowledge to give it a name.

All they knew was that when he appeared, he could suck the joy out of life
quicker than you could say "Woof woof."

A Black Dog can surprise you
with a visit for no apparent
reason or occasion.

He can make you look and feel older than your years.

While the rest of the world seems to be enjoying life, you can see it only through the Black Dog.

Activities that usually bring you pleasure may suddenly cease to.

If you have a Black Dog in
your life, it can dramatically
affect your appetite.

For some people, food becomes their only comfort, and they eat too much.
Others lose interest in it altogether.

A Black Dog can seriously affect your memory
and ability to concentrate.

Doing anything or going anywhere with him requires superhuman strength.

If your Black Dog follows you to a social occasion, there's a good chance he will sniff out whatever confidence you have and chase it away.

People who have a Black Dog in their lives
often fear that someone will find out.
They fear being judged or talked about,
or having responsibilities taken away.

They develop incredible reserves for putting on a brave, happy face, becoming like magicians who constantly pull rabbits out of hats to please the crowd.

The irony of it is, they wouldn't do magic tricks to cover up epilepsy, a heart attack, or diabetes.

A Black Dog can
make you think and say
negative things.

He can make you irritable, unreasonable, and generally difficult to be around.

A Black Dog will think nothing of taking away your love
and burying your intimacy.

When you're irritable, exhausted, and brimming with self-doubt, the Black Dog likes nothing more than to visit you in the wee hours of the morning and remind you of these things.

There are different degrees of feeling when you have a
Black Dog in your life. At one end of the scale you may feel sad,
flat, teary, or blue, and at the other, you are devoid of feeling altogether,
and life is overwhelmingly difficult.

If left unchecked, a Black Dog can become a serious problem. It gets bigger and likes to hang around all the time.

Occasionally you may find the energy to take him on and, hopefully, send him running.

But depending on the severity and size of your Black Dog,
he may come out on top, and getting up again will seem futile.

It's not unlike getting into
the ring with a professional
wrestler. If you don't like
getting hurt, it feels safest staying
down. That can become a big
problem, because you never get
out of the ring.

People understandably like to distance themselves from pain, be it physical or mental.
It's not uncommon for people to treat their Black Dog with a repeated dose of self-medication,

Left to his own devices, a Black Dog will take you to a place where you feel totally isolated from everything and everyone.

He may not rest until he has hijacked all aspects of your life and
made you question what the point of that life is.

But a Black Dog should never be allowed to get that far.

The surest way to put him back in his kennel is to seek professional help and get the proper diagnosis.

You will quickly discover that there are many different breeds
of Black Dog affecting millions of people from all walks of life.
The Black Dog is an equal-opportunity mongrel.

You will also learn that there are many different ways to treat a Black Dog, but there is no such thing as a quick fix or magic pill. Medication may be one part of an approach for some, but for others there might be a different method altogether.

Making a Black Dog "begone" is all about management—it requires different approaches and disciplines for different people and circumstances.

Learning not to be afraid of a Black Dog and teaching him a few new tricks of your own can be quite rewarding.

A Black Dog feeds on stress and fatigue;
the more stressed you get, the louder he barks.

It's important to learn how to rest properly and quiet your mind.
Yoga, meditation, and being in nature can help shut out the dog.

A Black Dog is fat and lazy; he wants you to lie on your bed and feel sorry for yourself. He hates exercise, mostly because it makes you feel better. When you least feel like moving, that's when you should move the most.

So go for a walk or run and leave the mutt behind.

Keeping a mood journal can be very useful.
Getting your thoughts on paper is highly liberating and often insightful.

It sounds obvious, but simply writing down what you are grateful for—
no matter how big or small—can help change the bleakest outlook for the better.

Work out a symbol for ranking how you feel each day—
it's a good way to keep track of the Dog.

The most important thing to remember is that no matter how bad it gets,

if you take the right steps, Black Dog days can and will pass.

No one would ever say he was grateful for having a Black Dog in his life.
But a negative experience can often help you find a more positive one.

Reevaluating and simplifying your life can only be beneficial.

Learning to acknowledge and even embrace your problems
can have surprisingly good outcomes.

It is possible that a Black Dog may always
be a part of your life, but with patience, humor,
knowledge, and discipline, even the worst
Black Dog can be made to heel.

I know — I've been living with one for
nearly twenty years.

The Beginning

SUGGESTED READING

Elkins, Rita. *Depression & Natural Medicine.* Orem, Utah: Woodland Publishing, 2001.

Kabat-Zinn, Jon. *Wherever You Go, There You Are: Mindfulness Meditation in Everyday Life.* New York: Hyperion, 2005.

O'Connor, Richard. *Undoing Depression: What Therapy Doesn't Teach You and Medication Can't Give You.* Boston: Little, Brown, 1997.

Parker, Gordon. *Dealing with Depression: A Commonsense Guide to Mood Disorders.* Crows Nest, New South Wales: Allen & Unwin, 2005.

Robertson, Joel with Tom Monte. *Natural Prozac: Learning to Release Your Body's Own Antidepressants.* New York: HarperCollins Publishers, 1997.

Sheffield, Anne. *Depression Fallout: The Impact of Depression on Couples and What You Can Do to Preserve the Bond.* New York: Quill, 2003.

Solomon, Andrew. *Noonday Demon: An Atlas of Depression.* New York: Scribner, 2001.

Styron, William. *Darkness Visible: A Memoir of Madness.* New York: Vintage Books, 1992.

Yapko, Michael D. *Breaking the Patterns of Depression.* New York: Doubleday, 1997.

HELPFUL WEB SITES

http://depression.about.com

www.beyondblue.org.au

www.blackdoginstitute.org.au

www.dbsalliance.org

www.jedfoundation.org

www.learningmeditation.com

www.moodgym.anu.edu.au

www.nami.org

www.nimh.nih.gov/healthinformation/depressionmenu.cfm

www.nlm.nih.gov/medlineplus/depression.html

www.nmha.org

www.undoingdepression.com

ACKNOWLEDGMENTS

I decided to create this book not so much as a self-help book but more as a visual articulation of what it is like to suffer from depression. I am not a psychologist, a psychiatrist, or a specialist in the field. I have merely had the unfortunate experience of suffering from what I unaffectionately call a Black Dog, the visual ambassador for the condition.

He is an omnipresent, foul-weather fiend who permeates everything like a drop of ink in a glass of water. My wish is that you can share this book with partners, parents, siblings, friends, and even doctors and therapists. It is a visual tool that may help you or someone you know.

I would like to thank all the people who have supported me in the process of making this book.

Thank you to my wonderful wife, Ainsley, who has stood by me with unconditional love, patience, humor, and support. To my daughters, Abby and Luca, for bringing me so much joy and being undoubtedly the best natural antidepressant I've ever had. My dearest family and friends, who have given so much love, encouragement, and support: thank you. To my literary agents, Pippa Masson, Fiona Inglis, Louise Thurtell, and the staff at Curtis Brown, who believed in this project and signed me up. To Jill Wran, who introduced me to Curtis Brown. To my publishers, Alex Craig at Pan Macmillan Australia and Chris Schillig at Andrews McMeel, for having the courage to buy and produce this book.

To Professor Gordon Parker and the staff at the Black Dog Institute for the fantastic work they do. Gordon, your belief, support, and enthusiasm made this book fly. Annie Schwebel at Mandarin Design, thank you so much for giving me a studio to work out of, and for your encouragement, creative advice, and technical pearls of wisdom. To David Hutton for his support and his InDesign know-how. To Kathrin Ayer, for taking the time to teach me how to illustrate in Photoshop. Thank you to the digital group at M&C Saatchi's for building the Web site www.ihadablackdog.com.

A really small, begrudging thank-you to my Black Dog; without you, this book would have not been possible — bad dog!

Everyone's path to recovery is different. If you are reading this book and have a Black Dog in your life, never, ever give up the fight; a Black Dog can be beaten. As Winston Churchill said, "If you find yourself going through hell, keep going." I wish you only peace and that you may find the quality and consistency of life that we all deserve.

Matthew Johnstone